REA

REPORTING THE UNIVERSE

**THE
WILLIAM E. MASSEY SR.
LECTURES IN THE
HISTORY OF AMERICAN
CIVILIZATION**

E. L. DOCTOROW

E. L. DOCTOROW

REPORTING THE UNIVERSE

**HARVARD
UNIVERSITY
PRESS**
CAMBRIDGE,
MASSACHUSETTS
LONDON,
ENGLAND
2003

REPORTING THE UNIVERSE

E. L. DOCTOROW

Library of Congress Cataloging-in-Publication Data

Doctorow, E. L., 1931–
    Reporting the universe / E.L. Doctorow.
        p. cm. — (The William E. Massey Sr. lectures in the history of
        American civilization ; 2000)
    ISBN 0-674-00461-2 (alk. paper)
    1. Doctorow, E. L., 1931–   2. Novelists, American—20th century—
Biography.   I. Title.   II. Series.

PS3554.O3 Z475 2003   2002032742
813′.54—dc21
[B]

CONTENTS

REPORTING THE UNIVERSE

E. L. DOCTOROW

The writer . . . believes all that can be thought can be written . . . In his eyes a man is the faculty of reporting, and the universe is the possibility of being reported.
　　　　　　　　　　　　　　—*Ralph Waldo Emerson*

These lines come of an earlier time in American letters, when the word *universe* did not evoke thoughts of the Big Bang but only meant . . . everything.

As the poet, essayist, Transcendentalist, and lapsed preacher Ralph Waldo Emerson conceives it, we are not about a fixed discoverable universe, but one constantly adjusting to the human inquiry. The universe as the possibility of being reported suggests endless ascription, infinite surprise.

Finally, the faculty of reporting and the possibility of being reported comprise the phenomenal crisis of human consciousness—which Emerson views with fascination as our great glory.

To report the universe is, in any age, a brazen inten-

1

tion, a kind of gnosticism, in fact, which asserts that the only contestants are the universe and the unenslaved mind. And tenable or not—recent literary critical theory would say not—the assertion is also hotly political because it is so freewheeling, so democratic. The writer in Emerson's definition is necessarily independent of all the aggregate communal fictions that may support and sustain him. All proprieties that govern the conduct of everyone around him come under his eye. Church, government, society, family, are all up for examination. He may choose to believe what his church teaches, he may choose to honor the government that rules him, he may choose to go about as a member of his society and write with respect of the hierarchies and customs of his family life, but an obligation does not exist. He will always be a loose cannon.

To people in power around the world uncensored books are unauthorized weapons. Certainly this is the conviction in countries outside the Western democracies, where under various forms of tight rule, secular or religious, writers have been and continue to be exiled, jailed, tortured, assassinated, and disappeared, the profession of politics being the other one which teaches its practitioners that reality is amenable to any construction placed upon it.

Emerson's idea of the writer goes right to the heart of the American metaphysic. He is saying we don't have the answers yet. It is a pragmatic thing to say. He knows he is at a culminant point in literary history, where the right of authorship has devolved from gods and their prophets and their priests to everyone. If the universe is the possibility of being reported, there is no end in sight to the variable genius of human character and the full expression of human capacity. A true democracy endows itself with a multiplicity of voices and assures the creation of a self-revising consensual reality that inches forward over the generations to a dream of truth.

Our problem, as contemporary writers who shy away instinctively from grand programs for ourselves, is that Emerson's lines were inspired by the work of Goethe. Goethe was a polymath with a scholarly appetite for botany, optics, philosophy, meteorology, and sin, among other interests. Since his time, knowledge has progressed and organized itself into disciplines, each with its own specialists and its own vocabulary.

The poet and the writer of fiction today fall outside this system—we are nothing if not generalists, and though we are known to wander into the lands of the scientists, for example, it is not with the same natural authority that someone of Goethe's era could assume when anyone who looked at bugs was an entomologist and everyone who pondered the night stars was an astronomer.

The fiction writer, or the poet, of today assumes a more modestly hopeful role in this society, like someone with a green card. We writers are exemplars of print culture, one of the minor forms of modern communication. We are a cottage industry in a post-industrial world. Our voices are constricted by the censorship of the marketplace. The entertainment behemoths that finance us are finding us a bad investment. The public libraries that stock our work have given over rooms to the Internet, videotapes, audiotapes, and music CDs.

But beyond our position in this business culture, and apart from the intimidations of the modernist project which by the application of science and technology to human problems has brought us such benefits of health and prosperity as were only dreamt of by our ancestors, we know that in order to survive we must keep secret whatever grand engagements with the universe we may posit for our work. We are not like Europeans in the nineteenth century given to the Romantic self-enlargement of our feelings. We observe the ironic national style of self-presentation if we are not to be booed off the stage. We know the enterprise of writing gives no warrants. The few monumental works that change our thinking, our seeing—Kafka, Beckett, in our time—rise from the chatter of what is temporal, imitative, foolish, and easily forgettable. The idea of society inching forward to a consensual reality, a dream of truth, does not guarantee to any one of us more than an incidental role, say as a worker in an ant colony. Nor does Emerson's cosmological vision square with what we know of ourselves, that we respond as much to the books we inherit as we do to the universe. We can't ignore the conversation that goes on among works of art, every book, however original, replying to an earlier book—the artists of every genre responding not only to the life around them but to the work that has gone on before. And then there is trans-genre adap-

around you the idea that you are still visibly the person you once were.

Of course, in the beginning, when you start out, you can know nothing of this. You are alive only to the great, if problematical, glory of your own consciousness.

CHILDHOOD OF A WRITER

I was given the name Edgar because my father loved the work of Edgar Allan Poe. Actually he liked James Fenimore Cooper too—in fact he liked a lot of bad writers—but I am consoled because Poe is our greatest bad writer. Just a few years ago I said to my aged mother, "Did you and Dad realize you were naming me after an alcoholic, drug-addicted, delusional paranoid with strong necrophiliac tendencies?" "Edgar," she replied, "that's not funny."

Of course as a child I was aware of none of this, nor of the fact that Poe, with the American nation in full bloom all around him, detested its democratic masses, preferring the aristocratic torment of his own solipsistic mind, which he projected as the dungeons, caskets, airless rooms, and other stultifying containers of his tales. In time I too would come to love this brilliant hack, this impoverished visionary, this contentious critic embattled in the literary life of his day. An immigrant New Yorker, with a palpable distaste for New England literary Brahmins, he went his own resentful way as a poet of lost loves and psychologist of the perverse. But in my childhood all I knew was that my parents had named me after a writer so famous that he was included in the deck of *Authors,* a popular card guessing game.

Naming is profoundly important, every name carrying an injunction and so, if coordinate enough with other circumstances of life, a fate. Not in my case, fortunately, to take drugs or to drink myself blind. But along with my literary name I found myself in a household of books, shelves of them, my parents' books, my older brother's books, the books my mother brought home from the rental library in the corner drugstore. And then there were the books I myself brought in by the armful every week from the New York Public Library branch on Washington Avenue in the Bronx.

When at the age of eight I was hospitalized with a burst appendix, I was given a new kind of book just then coming out, a book that could fit into your pocket, a pocket book or paperback that cost only twenty-five cents. Not knowing myself to be on the verge of death, I read in the interstices of my deliriums *Bring 'Em Back Alive* by Frank Buck, a scurrilous self-promoting white supremacist zoo supplier; *Bambi* by a bloodless Austrian writer named Felix Salten, as only someone bloodless could have written that insipid tale of a deer; then a not entirely reputable novel of Eastern mysticism by James Hilton, *Lost Horizon,* my introduction to the idea of a nonmaterialistic and therefore quite boring heaven on earth; and finally *Wuthering Heights,* a novel about adult matters which did not interest me. These were among the first ten titles released by Pocket Books, a new idea in American publishing stolen from the Europeans, and I still have them and remember their being placed on my bedside table by my pale wan worried mother and father as amulets to see me through it, whose love for their wretched sick child comes back to me at this advanced age—that light we live in and see by, if we're lucky, but only come to see, not when in our shared adulthood with our parents neither we nor they particularly remember it, but after their death, when that is what keeps living, that steady and irreducible light.

How understandable it is that in my early twenties,

out of the army, married with a child of my own, I hungrily sought and found employment as an editor with another publisher of mass paperback books, New American Library—the Signet line, the Mentor line— in what turned out to be the heyday of the mass market paperback, by then seventy-five cents or as much as a dollar and a quarter for the thick ones. I was cool enough not to reveal my larcenous excitement in having all these books to hand, and in getting paid to find and read good books and buy the rights and print up a hundred thousand, say, of a good obscure first novel, give it a jazzy cover, and ship it out to all the airports in the country, all the drugstores and railroad stations, for people to buy for pocket change in those days when you could find a consequential mass market book, not a genre romance, not an assembly-line techno-thriller, but a book—Pasternak's *Doctor Zhivago,* Ralph Ellison's *Invisible Man*—"Good Reading for the Masses" as the publisher promised, of the kind my parents intended me to have when I was in the hospital in danger of dying.

I was sent off to the suburb of Pelham Manor to convalesce in a quiet stately home, the domain of a quiet stately aunt, she, and her home, teaching me the necessary and sufficient conditions of a life of calmness, of soft-spoken speech. These were: space, live-in servants, clean windows with the sunlight shining through, and trees and grass and a flower garden outside the windows, none of which were available to my parents in their Bronx flat, home also to my mother's unemployed brother, a musician, the once successful leader of a swing orchestra, and my ancient grandmother, who was given to spells of madness. My parents, though united in their love for me and for my older brother, were otherwise in perpetual and highly vocal disagreement about how to survive in the Depression, the qualities of character it demanded . . . and whatever the benefits of my home life, peacefulness and the calm address were not among them. In my loyalty to my family, and possibly a subliminal fascination with the clutch of disparate personalities I lived among, all of them exemplars of the vivid communication, demonstrators of the powers to be achieved from abutting the Latin and the Anglo-Saxon, and with rare and so all the more effective recourse to the Yiddish, I felt estranged and possibly neglected in such suburban comfort and peace and quiet as my gentle aunt provided, and so took to the bookshelves of my cousin, away at college with her children's library left behind, and ploughed through the collected Oz novels of L. Frank Baum. A few years ago I read that Baum was a Communist, and that the Oz stories can be read as an allegory of communist idealism, the godlike Wizard being an admitted fraud, a temporary expedient, a ruling vanguard, you see, with the power really residing in the people if they would only come to realize it, though it takes a bit of traveling to get there . . . an interpretation I would have found quite useless had I known of it, especially as I was reading the book in the comfortable home of my aunt and uncle, he, I should say, a rock-ribbed Republican of such probity as hardly to countenance in his home a work of inflammatory literature directed at his own daughter. Additionally, I am skeptical. I don't question the fact of Baum's politics or even his intentions, though we know by now that an author's intentions are hardly reliable measures of his accomplishments; but the images of which the Oz books are constructed are so vivid and original as virtually to wipe out any referential meanings that would

arise. Besides which, my cousin, in whose room I slept, was a fancier of dogs, she had raised a champion Kerry blue terrier, its blue ribbons went around the four walls of the room like a cove molding, and on her shelves along with Baum were several of the canine novels of Albert Payson Terhune, whose hero dogs always managed to save their owners' wealthy mansions from the depredations of evil interlopers, usually African American. These tales, so in sync with the prevailing social attitudes in the town of Pelham Manor, county of Westchester, 1939, were not visibly racist to the unraised consciousnesses of white God-fearing circumspection in my aunt's peaceful house. Terhune's volumes far outnumbered those of L. Frank Baum, and what I took from them was something else entirely, the literary possibilities in attributing human emotions to an animal.

Back home, and more or less on my feet again, I took out of the public library the two great dog novels of Jack London, published together for my convenience in one sturdy library binding, *Call of the Wild* and *White Fang*, the one about a civilized dog who is kidnapped and enslaved as a sled-husky in the Yukon and, under the brutal pressures of human masters, finds freedom and self-realization in reverting to the primeval wolf ways of his remote ancestry, the other about a savage wolf who, under the ministrations of a decent human being, becomes a civilized human-friendly dog. He was nothing, Jack London, if not a writer who knew a good formula when he found one. On tales such as these he became the most popular writer in America, and he is still widely read around the world, though he sits at literature's table below the salt while the more sophisticated voices of modernist and postmodernist irony conduct the conversation.

The tests and trials to which Buck, the dog in *Call of the Wild,* is subjected, and the way he meets them and learns and grows in moral stature, make Buck a round character, while the human beings in the book are, in their constant one-note villainy, flat. That is irony too, a fine irony. Furthermore, this little speed-readers' novel, written at the level of a good pulp serial, is in fact a parody of the novel of sentimental education, not only because the hero is a dog, but because his education decivilizes him, turns him back into the wild creature of his primordial ancestry. I appreciate that now, but then I only knew Jack London was different from the picture-book writer Aesop, he was not tiresome as Aesop was, he took animals seriously, granting them complex character as the veterinarily incorrect Aesop never did. The moral of the Jack London book was not something you knew already without having to be instructed. But it was there and it was resonant with my own life. Every day, it seemed, old men knocked on the front door to ask my mother for money to help bring Jews out of Europe. Playing with my friends in the park, I had to watch out for older boys who swept up from the East Bronx to take at knifepoint our spaldines and whatever pocket change we were carrying. My father, the proud owner of a music shop in the old Hippodrome theater at Sixth Avenue and Forty-Third Street, a man who knew the classical repertoire inside out and stocked music that nobody else had, a man whom the great artists of the day consulted for their record purchases, lost his store in the "little" Depression of 1940. My ancient grandmother, growing more and more insane each day, now ran away to wander the streets until the police found her and brought her home. We were broke, what the newspapers called war clouds were growing darker and more ominous, my brother was of freshly minted draft age, and *The Call of the Wild,* this mordant parable of the thinness of civilization, the savagery bursting through as the season changed in the Bronx and a winter of deep heavy snows, like the snows of the Yukon, fell upon us, the whole city muffled and still, made me long to be in the wild, loping at the head of my pack, ready to leap up and plunge my incisors into the throats of all who would harm me or my family.

At one point I must have realized the primordial power belonged not only to the dog, or not in fact to the dog, because around this time—I was perhaps nine years old—I decided I was a writer. It was a clear conviction, not even requiring a sacred vow; I assumed the identity with grace, as one slips on a jacket or sweater that fits perfectly. It was such a natural assumption of my mind that for several years I felt no obligation actually to write anything. My convalescence had left me flabby, out of shape, with less energy for running around. I was more disposed than ever to read or listen to radio stories, and I was now reading not only to find out what happened next but with that additional line of inquiry of the child writer who is yet to write: *How is this done?* It is a kind of imprinting. We live in the book as we read it, yes, but we run with the author as well—this wild begetter of voices, this voice of voices, this noble creature of the wild whose linguistic lope over any sort of terrain brings it into being.

Understandably, in a season of gloom and menace, I soon achieved a taste for horror stories—Poe, naturally, W. W. Jacobs, Mary Shelley, Saki, and the even bloodier vendors of the comic book tales. My father was not too distracted with worry to notice this, and he was not without a sense of humor. He handed me a book from the bookcase in my grandparents' apartment when we were visiting one Sunday afternoon: "Here, since you like all that horror stuff, here's one called *The Green Hand*. Sounds good and horrible to me." While all the grown-ups were having tea I sat in a corner and opened this book, and of course it wasn't a horror story about some disembodied, gangrenous green hand, it was a novel about a novice aboard a sailing ship, a *greenhand*. So by means of my father's trickery I fell to reading nothing but sea stories. That particular volume was one of a set of sea novels my grandfather had—*The*

Wreck of the Grosvenor, Captain Marryat, Moby-Dick, and so on. I was to go through them all.

My grandfather had a personal library of books he'd picked up over the years in various kinds of promotions: book sets and encyclopedias, multi-volume histories like the *Harper's History of the Civil War,* masterworks of all ages in uniform editions with titles like *The World's Great Orations.* My grandfather was a printer who had come here from Russia as a young man in 1885. In those days books were premiums you collected coupons for when you bought other things, including the daily newspaper. And all the immigrants who were trying to catch up as fast as possible collected these books. But he'd always been a great reader, my grandfather, and among his few precious possessions that he brought over with him in steerage were his books in Russian and in Yiddish. It was from my grandfather that I first heard the name Tolstoy—Lev Tolstoy he called him. One day he recounted to me Tolstoy's not exactly appropriate story for a child's ear, *The Death of Ivan Ilyich,* which describes in detail what it feels like to die. But he was right, I was fascinated. Another time he made me a present of one of his books, Tom Paine's

The Age of Reason, a scornful dismissal of biblical fundamentalism. "My own mind is my church," Paine says, announcing his blasphemous Deism. It was this book among other rowdy acts that made the great writing hero of the American Revolution an embarrassment to the new government. My grandfather presented me with his copy around the time I was studying for my bar mitzvah. For among other tensions in my wonderful family was an irresolvable religious conflict, the generations of men, my grandfather, my father, being skeptics, the women, my grandmothers, my mother, being to one degree or another observant, keepers of dietary laws, lovers of the Sabbath, candle lighters, fasters on the High Holy Days, and so on.

Nowadays educators, psychologists speak of the ideal of the enriched childhood, and I see how enriched mine was amidst these hard-living adults who struggled to pay the rent and put food on the table. But how could I or any of us know how enriching it all was—it was life, that's all, it was normal, feverishly expressive burgeoning life. Our under-financed household was filled with music, not only my father's extensive record collection, to which, if I was careful handling the breakable 78s in their sleeves, I had unrestricted access, but my mother's pianistics, for she was a consummate musician, the daughter of musicians, whose disquieted soul found solace in the most tempestuous pieces of Chopin—the Revolutionary Etude, for example, that thunderously rolling earthquake of a composition. My older brother played jazz piano and organized a band that rehearsed in the front parlor also known as the sunroom. Music of all kinds and periods filled my home and my head. And though I never took to it as a discipline, having dismayed everyone within hearing when I sat down to practice my piano lessons, somehow the difference between notes on a staff and words on a page must have elided in my child's mind, which may be why in my working life those aroused mental states from which books begin are as likely to be evoked by a phrase in music as by the music I hear in words.

It is true also that everyone in my family seemed to be a good storyteller, every one of them without exception. They were persons to whom interesting things seemed to happen. The events they spoke of were most often of a daily, ordinary sort, but when composed and narrated, of great importance and meaning. Of course when you bring love to the person you're listening to, a story has to be interesting, and in one sense the challenge to a professional writer of books is to overcome the disadvantage of not being someone the reader knows and loves. But apart from that, the family of storytellers I listened to must have had a very firm view of themselves in the world. Otherwise they could not have done it so well. They were authorities of their own lives. They were strong enough presences in their own minds to trust that people would attend to them when they spoke. In fact their narratives were often accounts of their struggle for recognition of the worth they felt in themselves . . . or briefs against the lack of recognition they were receiving from others. There was no end to the varieties of myths they could construct from the realities of their relationships with one another.

Without realizing it I was spending a good part of my childhood listening quite carefully to the conversations of adults, even on those occasions when I was not known to be listening. And I particularly attended to the use of words at moments of high emotion, even when that emotion, anger, for instance, was directed at

Homer. As in Genesis. This was reported to me as the Holophrastic theory of language and the image provided was of a star, the points being where we are today, the center being of that early linguistically imploded time. I don't know who came up with this idea or if it is still bandied about in seminars or if it has gone out of fashion or been modified to compatibility by cultural studies constructionists. But verifiable or not, it satisfies me because it explains why even as we live in an age that is scientifically oriented, even as we hold to the values of empiricism, demanding of our propositions that they be tested and of our legal cases that they rest on demonstrable evidence, our modern minds are still structured for storytelling. Facts may change, evolve, they do so all the time, but stories find their way to the unchanging core of things. People think naturally in terms of conflict and its resolution and in terms of character undergoing events, and of the outcomes of events being not at all sure, and therefore suspenseful . . . and the whole thing done moreover from a confidence of narrative that must belong to us and to our brains as surely as we are predisposed to the protocols of grammar.

If you want to test this particular proposition you cannot do better than to read some works of oral history. I remember reading from one collection—I don't have the title to hand—of pieces by women who settled on the Kansas frontier in the nineteenth century where they and their families were subjected to floods, droughts, plagues of locusts, and a series of topical ailments, most prominently ague, which we would call malaria. There's a line I've never forgotten from one of these women speaking of a neighboring family:

When Mr. Briggs was so with it [the ague] that Mrs. Briggs had to cut the wood, she put the baby behind him on the corded bedstead where his shivering joggled the baby off to sleep.

This writer knew, this neighbor of the Briggs', what that master theorist of fiction, Flaubert, had articulated as a kind of discovery: that the way to make an object in fiction exist is to have it worked upon by another object. What makes things come into being is their transaction. Mr. Briggs' illness exists because he shivers, the bed exists because he lies upon it, and the sleeping baby exists because his father's malarial convulsions rock the bedstead. But this writer knew more—and so we learn from Mrs. Briggs' action a good deal of her character, her enterprise in using even her husband's illness in their daily struggle for survival on the prairie. We know this life is harsh. We can imagine from this sentence alone the homemade nature of the house, perhaps even what things look like outside the house, and in fact we may derive from it the entire character of life on the American frontier in the mid-nineteenth century.

For all of that, though, books are books, meaning that unlike people they can detail the whole three hundred and sixty degrees from birth to death. And who in the world can tell a story as well as Mark Twain and Charles Dickens? I found *David Copperfield* in my parents' library—two volumes in the flexible black bindings of the Harvard Classics, the five-foot shelf assembled by Charles W. Eliot just for me. Others of Dickens' works I pulled from the shelves of the public library branch on Washington Avenue. It was a bit of a walk from my house to the library, and fittingly enough, to get there I had to pass a bread-baking factory from which issued the delicious smells of fresh baking rye and pumpernickel. The copy of *Great Ex-*

great work—only Sid could have made a home for himself in London, the others never. Twain does set *The Prince and the Pauper* in sixteenth-century England, but that story turns out to be the most precise symbolic presentation of the democratic ideal imaginable because the two boys, Tom Canty and the Prince, are seen to be interchangeable, each one, pauper and prince, functioning quite well as the other, and what is being said is anti-European and anti-monarchical—that a society of class distinctions is essentially a fraud.

But with what a thrill of recognition I read my own feelings as they were rendered in *Tom Sawyer:* Tom's aversion to soap and water; his keen interest in the insect forms of life; his not always kind attention to dogs and cats; how he found solace from the unjust judgment of an Aunt Polly by dreaming of running away; how he loved Becky Thatcher, the sort of simpering little blonde I too fell for in grade school; how he did the absolutely right thing in taking her punishment at school to protect her. But most of all, without consciously realizing it, I had to have recognized the truth of the taxonomic world Tom Sawyer lived in, because it was so in accord with my own, a world of two dis-

Among Virginia Woolf's collected essays is a talk she gave at a school entitled "How Should One Read a Book?" "Try to become [the author]," she advises.

Be his fellow worker and accomplice . . . the chapters of a novel are an attempt to make something as formed and controlled as a building: but words are more impalpable than bricks . . . Perhaps the quickest way to understand the elements of what a novelist is doing is not to read, but to write; to make your own experiment with the dangers and difficulties of words.

And so I did, finally, get around to writing, after the war had begun, and my brother was off somewhere overseas, and my father, working now as a salesman, read the news each evening, buying up every paper he could get his hands on. I was in junior high school, sometimes called middle school, seventh to ninth grade. Little pennants with blue stars had appeared in all the windows of the neighborhood, and sometimes gold stars as well, and the newsreels in the movie houses showed the tanks rumbling, the bombs falling, the ships' guns firing, while I, having been named after Poe, took to writing in the hermetic tradition, setting my stories in dungeons or dark houses that lacked central heating. They began with lines like "The cell was dark and dank."

After my Poe period I lay fallow for a while. Ideas came to me as sudden arousals of the brain, cerebral excitements that I would attempt to convert to a plot or situation, trying to write it and then giving up after a paragraph or two and going out to play ball. Also, in those days there was a lot of radio drama, afternoon and evening, always with introductory music to set the mood. And so I'd get a vague inspiration of one sort or another and then put a record on the phonograph, some music I felt was dramatic, an opera overture, a jazz tune, and imagine it as the beginning of a scene or episode for a radio story that was going to come to me at any minute.

It is possible that my writing clock had been set back by the seismic shock of puberty, a whole new way of thinking or obsessing that only tied in with the idea of writing on such occasions as my discovery of *Mademoiselle de Maupin* by Théophile Gautier, a racy French novel that, as I read it even in circumspect translation, made my heart pound and my ears turn red. Around this time the war ended, my brother came home un-scathed, and he resumed his undergraduate career at City College, today known as CUNY, where he en-rolled in a writing class and proceeded to write a novel during the course of a winter on his portable typewriter each night at the kitchen table. It told of the peacetime adjustment problems of some army veterans returning to their old neighborhoods. This in fact is what all the postwar novels seemed to be about, and my brother subsequently abandoned his effort. But seeing him tap-ping away late into the night had its effect on me. Here was our own family war hero proposing the act of writ-ing as the serious endeavor of a responsible adult, the pages accumulating right before my eyes.

A year or so later I found myself a student at the Bronx High School of Science, an institution filled with insufferably brilliant children, some of whom were quite convinced, correctly as it turned out, that they would in time win the Nobel Prize in physics. Meanwhile, instead of doing the assigned lab work, I was reading Kafka's stories, *Metamorphosis* and the rest, and hanging out with the other displaced humanists in a little corner office where *Dynamo,* the school's literary magazine, was published. Inevitably it published something of mine, a short story entitled "The Beetle," my teenage homage to the master's really cool use of entomological self-defamation. But that was hardly enough to satisfy what was now almost a physical need to write, and so when I had the opportunity to enroll in a journalism class for the usual English course credit, I jumped at it.

There are, to tell the truth, fewer epiphanies in life than there are in literature—I mean in the Joycean sense of the term, those moments of inexorable moral definition that predict a life, a fate. I suppose I am fortunate to be able to identify one, retrospectively, in my life. What happened was this: our high school journalism teacher ordered us to go out into the world and conduct an interview. I threw myself into the assignment, exercising initiative, working hard, and I turned in an interview with the stage doorman at Carnegie Hall. He was a German Jewish refugee, a camp survivor, the only one in his family, a prematurely aged sweet-tempered man with rheumy eyes, who wore an old double-breasted blue serge jacket, unbuttoned, and baggy brown pants. Each evening he came to work with his lunch in a paper bag and a thermos of hot tea.

He drank his tea in the old-world way by putting a cube of sugar between his teeth and sipping the tea through the sugar. His life had been shattered but he had spirit, and he knew the repertoire, he could speak knowledgeably about composers and musicians. Over the years he'd become a fixture in the place, and all the great recitalists, Horowitz, Rubinstein, Jascha Heifitz, knew him and called him by his first name, Karl. Karl the Doorman.

My teacher was so impressed with the piece that she decided it should run in the school newspaper. She called me up to her desk after class and said she wanted one of the photography students to go down to Carnegie Hall and take the old doorman's picture to go along with the story. I had not anticipated this degree of enthusiasm. I said I didn't think that was possible—Karl would never let his picture be taken.

"Why?" she asked.

"Well, he's very shy."

"How shy can he be?" she said. "He talked to you, didn't he?"

"Well not exactly," I said. "There is no Karl the Doorman. I made him up."

Once more in my child's life, I had yielded the high

ground to the other life form. My teacher would bring up the big guns, a trip to the principal's office, a note to my parents, before she was through. But it had seemed to me so much better to make up that stage doorman than actually to go through the tedious business of interviewing someone. If there wasn't a Karl the Doorman, there should have been. And what about Kafka, after all, he wrote from his imagination about things that weren't verifiable from the real everyday world, but they were true!

Not that I tried to defend myself. Today I would of course explain to the teacher that I had done no more than what journalists have always done.

But I have since thought about this incident. It is, I suppose, a novelist's story. It can stand as a kind of parable of the novelist's birth. For the practice has taught me that nothing I write will turn out well unless during the course of the writing I feel the same thrill of transgression I felt as I put together from my young life and times the images I needed for the invention of Karl the Stage Doorman at Carnegie Hall. I believe nothing of any beauty or truth comes of a piece of writing without the author's thinking he has sinned against something—propriety, custom, faith, privacy, tradition, political orthodoxy, historical fact, literary convention, or indeed, all the prevailing community standards together. And that the work will not be realized without the liberation that comes to the writer from his feeling of having transgressed, broken the rules, played a forbidden game—without his understanding or even fearing his work as a possibly unforgivable transgression.

Karl, of course, was of the same profession as the forbidding-looking guard in Kafka's *The Trial*, who stands at the door to The Law and who tells the poor supplicant at the end of his life that the door had been his to pass through had he tried. My doorman Karl stood at the door to The Music and addressed me unambiguously in my teen age and I thank God for him.

"Open it," he told me. "Go ahead, my boy, this door is intended for you. It's your door to open. Open it."

On an evening in September 1948, my parents escorted me to the awesome steel and green glass industrial cathedral known as Pennsylvania Station, where I said goodbye and took my coach seat for the overnight ride to Kenyon College in Gambier, Ohio. I had with me a small valise and a paper bag with two sandwiches and an apple. A footlocker would follow in a week or two via the Railway Express.

To this day I don't know how at age sixteen I had heard about Kenyon, its solid liberal arts curriculum, and especially the poet and New Critic who taught there, John Crowe Ransom. Perhaps an enlightened guidance counselor at Science High had told me about the school, perhaps I had read some of Ransom's poems. In any event, there I would proceed with the intention of majoring in English.

My father had taken out a bank loan to cover the year's tuition and room and board, which came to fifteen hundred dollars. The plan was for me to do well enough to make the Dean's List and apply for financial aid thereafter.

Kenyon had been a fashionable second-rate college in the Twenties and early Thirties, a watering hole for the wealthy sons of midwestern businessmen. In those days the students had an airfield for their private planes and the school fielded a polo team. By 1940 it had turned itself through the energies of a president named Gordon Chalmers into a real college, with a first-rate faculty built around Ransom and the philosopher Phillip Blair Rice. By 1948 it could boast of a student golden age that had included the poet Robert Lowell and the short story writer Peter Taylor. The poet and critic Randall Jarrell had been an instructor in the English department. The normal student population of five hundred was now over seven hundred, the G.I. bill having swelled the enrollment with veterans. A new enlightened admissions program had opened Kenyon's doors to students of public high schools of distinction in New York and Philadelphia.

This is not to say that I was entirely comfortable on my arrival. The campus was very beautiful with venerable ivy-covered college buildings in a style that might be called Western Reserve Oxonian set among the trees. Abruptly, and I thought without sufficient ceremony, I found myself reading Milton and Matthew Arnold. The campus was still under the social rule of eight fraternities, each with its own section of one of the three dormitories in the college park and its own lodge in the woods around Gambier. The fraternity upperclassmen marched down the Middle Path each Tuesday night singing their fraternity hymns. They wore white bucks and gray flannel trousers and sweaters in the school's royalist colors, purple and white. Prominently positioned on the campus was the ivied Church of the Holy Spirit, Episcopal, Kenyon being affiliated with that denomination. And all students regardless of their religion or lack of it were required to attend chapel on Sunday morning.

Drinking also seemed to be something of a requirement, though unwritten. Parties were frequent and the Dance Weekends had achieved notoriety as far east as Smith and Vassar. On party nights bathtubs were ceremoniously filled with gin and grapefruit juice, a drink known as Seabreeze. I remember once being held in an affectionate necklock by a drunken Deke who said to me with tears in his eyes: "All men are brothers. Don't matter if you're Episcopal, Presbyterian, Lutheran, or even a Baptist."

Fortunately I was not alone as an outsider. Those students who were not elected to a fraternity or who, like me, refused to accept election, were ghettoized as Independents and for the most part lived in Old Kenyon, the steepled original college building, constructed circa 1804. The Independents were housed in the center third of Old Kenyon known as Middle Kenyon. If you lived in Middle Kenyon you were a Mu Kap, a kind of fraternity man despite yourself.

The Mu Kaps were Jews and Catholics from the East, the first two black students ever admitted, poor country boys like my friend James Wright the poet, a sprinkling of gays, some foreign nationals, a long-haired premature Hippie or two, and a few boys given to social afflictions like shyness or acne. The only thing common to them all was the disposition to do well academically. It was this group, I was told by Professor Phil Rice, that kept him teaching at Kenyon. It was this group I was eventually to join, after being housed temporarily with other freshmen off the campus in barracks the college had set up to accommodate the swollen postwar enrollment.

Phil Rice was also the associate editor of the *Kenyon Review,* which was edited by Ransom. It was Rice's influence that opened the *Review*'s pages to the postwar European existentialist and Euro-centrist critics and poets. Rice was a brilliant teacher, a portly man never without a lit Camel in his fingers, whose smoke-thickened mumblings were written down by us in a secretarial fever. It was in thrall to Rice's courses in metaphysics and aesthetics and to those of his colleague Virgil Aldrich, a logician and ethicist, that I changed my major to philosophy.

I was still able to study poetry with John Ransom, of course. At this point he was no longer the unregenerate New Critical Agrarian—he had thawed out quite a bit by the time I arrived at Kenyon—but he taught his classes as a strict textualist, and the presumption was purely New Critical that a poem, and presumably a novel as well, had within it everything you needed to understand it, a kind of isolationist approach to literary texts that would nevertheless turn out to be invaluable training for a budding writer. It was scintillating to work as an exegete. I would in time write a thirty-five-page paper on Wordsworth's eight-line lyric "A Slumber Did My Spirit Seal." This was nothing unusual at Kenyon, where we did literary criticism the way they played football at Ohio State.

In February 1949, the spring semester of my freshman year, about a week before I was to move from my temporary quarters into Old Kenyon as an Independent, a fire broke out one Saturday night in the basement lounge of the Mu Kaps. It was almost immediately out of control. The nearest fire department was five miles away in the town of Mount Vernon. By morning the building was a ruin. Several students had been injured and nine students were missing, all of them from Middle Kenyon.

On Sunday morning we stood looking at what had been the architectural symbol of the school. Blue smoke rose from the ruins. It was not that long since we had seen in the newsreels the bombed rubble of buildings destroyed in World War II, and that was

Alumni House in the village of Gambier at the edge of the college park. Our physical separation from the rest of the school population rendered us signifiers of the disaster, a sort of living memorial to our dead friends. In some unconscious way we set about making an alternative college of our own. Our games were intense and almost invariably collegiate variations of the games we had played in the streets of our childhoods. We were competitive with one another and strove to write the best papers, come up with the best insights, the best grades. We were in fact making Kenyon in our own image, with as many claims to our school as the most traditional fraternity jocks. I established myself as each of us had to do, undergoing the crucial assertive process of self-definition in a constant stream of ideas and feelings, which, I would like to think, amounted to an incipient multiculturalist defiance, though I wouldn't have understood it as such. Nor would the others. We were of course aware of the sociology of the place, we were not fools, but it didn't seem to matter. A few of us had learned that by going to Mansfield, Ohio, forty miles to the north, every week to teach Sunday school to the children of Jewish families in a small Reform congregation, we could satisfy the compulsory chapel requirement. We all knew that our teachers respected us. Several of us were sought by the fraternities we disdained. Some of us played varsity sports. In no way were we denied the campus-wide opportunities or pursuits that erased the social division of college life. Yet for all of that, the structurally denominational, which is to say political, culture of the school was unchanged.

At this time in our country "atomic spies" were being arrested, writers were being interrogated by the House Un-American Activities Committee, Senator Joe McCarthy was discovering traitors in the State Department, and apparently it was now possible in the United States to commit crimes of thought. Loyalty oaths were required of state college professors, public school teachers, municipal clerks. Blacklists decimated the ranks of screen actors, directors, writers. It was the darkest period of the Cold War. On our idyllic campus we were read to by Robert Frost. We had available to us courses in Roman and ancient Greek history, Church history, but not twentieth-century Church history. I was able to read and discuss Conrad and Dostoyevsky without reference to their social or religious conservatism. The star of our political science syllabus was

Edmund Burke. T. S. Eliot was foremost among the major modern poets to be studied, with some discussion of his Anglo-Catholic medievalist ideals but not their anti-Semitic adornments. None of this was insidious or doctrinaire. Our teachers were honest, dedicated scholars. But it is the nature of a prevailing culture not to appear ideological, especially to its executors.

"Only connect," said E. M. Forster, another novelist I was reading, and that is what I must have been trying to do when, to get to the bottom of things, or the top, to connect everything, from the genial, passionately well meant denominational education given me at Kenyon to my childhood's dark image of European Christianity that I had brought with me on the Pennsylvania Railroad, I wrote a paper for my metaphysics course entitled "A Beginner Looks at God." The title was ironic, but I wanted also to dissociate myself proudly from those who had the credentials in this matter, not understanding at the time that all theology is the work of beginners, that even the greatest systematic studies of the acclaimed theologians cannot break through or scale the impenetrable unscalable wall of that subject. And not having yet read them I could not have known that these same theologians, in their eloquent, creative, and ardent investigations in search of God, almost invariably discover him, after all, in the very faiths into which they were born. Inevitably, that makes them, however poetic their ideas, however helpless or desperate their embrace of their faith, performers of a kind of celestial public relations that finally has little enough to do with the ground wars fought in the names of their religion and the politics by which it claims its sacred authority.

My own undergraduate conclusion was to come down on the side of the traditional skepticism of my father and his father before him, a position no more original than any other, and no more illuminating, as if religious issues in the world were, after all, exactly what they had been in my family—where the men were nonbelievers and the women pious keepers of the sacraments—a theoretical dispute among relatives, and in the case of my grandparents one of the forms of marital communication that bound them together for life.

Only connect. Now I feel well qualified to speak of godly matters, my credentials being those of a storyteller.

TEXTS THAT ARE SACRED,
TEXTS THAT ARE NOT

As a novelist I must necessarily stand outside the system of expertise that structures the intellectual life of our society. A novelist is a specialist in nothing, unendowed by discipline and therefore able to travel back and forth freely across the borders that demarcate disciplines. I can employ the concepts of science, the poetics of theology. I can speak as an anthropologist, a philosopher, a pornographer. I can employ the materials of history, I can report as a journalist, I can resort to confession, autobiography, myths, legends, dreams, hallucinations, and the mutterings of poor mad people in the street. All of these have equal weight as far as I am concerned. I will use all the words from every mode of thinking with the assurance that they can meld into a sensible composition. I believe so completely in fiction that I regard it as a mega-discipline, one that incorporates all others, blurs the genres, whips together fact and imagination, and at its best reasserts the authority of the single unaffiliated mind to render the world. Just as it did in ancient times, when the story was a knowledge system, indeed the primary means of organizing and storing knowledge—when fact was a function of visionary belief, and people created the stories that we read and are ruled by to this day. Our scripture, our God stories.

Literary practitioners are conservatives who cherish the ultimate structures of the human mind, who cultivate the universal disposition to think in stories, the very first means of knowing, the total discourse that antedates the special vocabularies of modern intelligence.

But for all its powers literature does not call upon followers. It is invariably bipolar, the doubt always immanent in the assertion, there is always a no inside the yes and a yes inside the no. It purveys moral complexity, paradox, irony, pathos, human failure, and the failure, comic or tragic, of human institutions. It is a mirror of the irresolute human soul. It says "This is how it feels, this is the truth of the felt life." In so doing it confounds simplistic belief, it resists the constriction of freedom that attaches to society's aggregate fictions which, by their inertia, instill a stupor of thought. But literature does not call upon followers.

I refer of course to literature since the Bronze and Iron ages. Because the ancestral literatures of those times, the sacred texts of our religions, by reason of their attributed authorship do call upon followers. The scriptures of Judaism, Christianity, and Islam were produced or revealed in those ages when stories were all people had—and when their invention was the word of God. Those residual communal texts that have made us who we are were hard-won instructions for survival and discoveries of the intellect that were configured illustratively, sometimes in verse, so as to be transmittable by memory from person to person, long before they came to be written. They gave counsel. They connected the present with the past. They bound the visible to the invisible. They distributed the suffering so that it could be borne. Like the stories of today, they made no distinction between fact and fiction, between ordinary communication and heightened language. But they were not self-conscious literary acts. All the modes of language which we now distinguish according to the situation we're in had not yet been devised.

Language was enchanted. And the very act of telling a story carried a presumption of truth.

The Hebrew Bible is clearly a redacted communal creation though attributed by the very religious in part to Moses. Muhammad too is considered an author though his words were written down by others—and Jesus' words, actions, and fate are reported upon by the gospelers with the same variable accounts and suspect objectivity we find in some of today's reporters. But in ancient times only God or his prophets could hold the esteemed title of author. The sacred texts of all religions based on Hebrew scripture have been communally amended, rewritten, commented upon, interpreted by rabbis, priests, imams, in order to transform religious apprehension into churches, unmediated awe into dogma, inchoate feeling into sacrament, brute expression into ethical commandment. But the authorship of God, through his intermediaries, is uncontested. And if a portion of a sacred text is illogical, opaque, self-contradictory, bipolar, enigmatic, God in his authorial perfection is not to be questioned, only we, his readers, for our inadequacies.

In the histories of civilizations the right of authorship has descended like a cleansing rain from the heavens to earth. Wars have been fought, orthodoxies have been thrown off, human consciousness has gone through revolutions, and human beings have been reconceived in freedom in order for this to happen. In a modern world deprived by rationalism and science of the comprehensive magic of a divinely conceived universe, all authors are recognized as mortal. And every story has to make it on its own.

When Bacon and Galileo insisted on putting claims of knowledge to the test with observation and experiment, storytelling as the prime means of understanding the world was so reduced in authority that today it is only children who continue to believe that stories are, by the fact of their being told, true. Children and fundamentalists.

Since September 11, 2001, I have been thinking about the ancient writings. Of course there are hard real-political understandings to apply to the rise of global terrorism. But taking our cue from Emerson we might describe the terror inflicted by the religiously brainwashed nihilists of Al Qaeda as arising from that part of the world where, for many people, the universe is not the possibility of being reported because it has been accounted for, attributed in its entirety now and forever to a Supreme Author.

It is inconceivable in an absolutist theocracy, a country run by religious dictate—it is inconceivable in any society where the answers are already given and the rules of life are inflexible and the authority for all thought is the ruling modality—that free expression and the multiplicity of witness can be anything but an abomination, a danger to the state or an affront to God, God, or the state, having done all the writing that was necessary for anyone, for all time.

And so the underlying conflict to come might be understood as between the old stories and the new, or between the fanatical readers of the old and the impertinent writers of the new, between the ancient revealed-as-divine writings and the writings of our later civilizations whose authors are mortal, multiple, and, while lacking any holy credential or indeed necessary exemption from evil of their own, are engaged in reporting the universe.

In the short run, I think, the intellectual satisfaction that came of doing criticism and philosophy at Kenyon put a damper on the instinctive feeling I had for fiction writing. The rigorous instruction I received in the forms and structures and tropes of literary composition was all analytical and perhaps induced a degree of self-consciousness about my own aspirations. The great philosophical questions were by turns thrilling and humbling. The philosophical categories were immediately and permanently useful, but it was all too easy to lose oneself in the philosophical diction. So that as relevant and invaluable as my education would turn out to be to my life as a writer, I would not settle down to write my first novel until I was years beyond graduation, married, a veteran myself, and in my late twenties. I did do some writing at Kenyon, but what I turned out was mere mental exercise. I had gone backward, away from that natural surging need to express something, anything, to something else—if not backward then certainly up to the regions of the brain, to calculation, study, research, to the conscious application of learning, all of it wrapped tightly in the longings of the ego.

The truth of the matter is that the creative act doesn't fulfill the ego but changes its nature. As you write you are less the person you ordinarily are—the situation confers strength. You learn to trust what comes to you unbidden. You learn to trust the act of writing itself. An idea, an image, a voice, comes to you as a discovery, and you don't possess what you write any more than the mountain climber possesses the mountain.

Writers write by trying to find out what it is they're writing. The artist Marcel Duchamp was once asked why he gave up painting: "Too much of it was filling in," he said. The worker in any medium had best give it up if he finds himself only filling in what has been previously declared and completed in his mind, a creative *fait accompli*. It is not that you have no intellect when you write. It is not that you have no convictions or beliefs. It is that nothing good will come of merely filling in what you already know. You must trust the act of writing to scan all the passions and convictions in your mind, but these must defer to the fortuitousness of the work, they must be of it. A book begins as an image, a sound in the ear, the haunting of something you don't want to remember, or perhaps a great endowing anger. But it is not until you find a voice for whatever is going on inside you that you can begin to make a coherent composition. The language you find precedes your intention or, if not, is sure to transform it.

By way of illustration I will dwell for a moment on how, accidentally, my first novel came to be written. After college, and after service in the Army of Occupation in Germany, I came home to write and found I could not. I constructed outlines for books, I researched subjects for books, I intended to write books. And none of them got written. At this time I found work as a professional reader for a film company. The job called for reading novels and preparing synopses for the film executives who didn't themselves have time to read, or perhaps couldn't read, but were on the lookout for stories that could be adapted for the screen. In these days, in the late Fifties, Westerns were very popular, and so it was given to me to cover one rotten Western after another. Despairing of my own failed efforts and the wretched pulp I was synopsizing, I thought of quitting. Then remembering Henry James's admonition to the writer—to be the person on whom nothing is lost—I decided that I could lie about the West better than any of the authors I was reading. I put a piece of paper in the typewriter and typed "Chapter One" at the top, just the way writers in the movies do it. I had no plan, no outline, no research. All I had was the impulse to parody. But I had happened upon a wonderful geography book, *The Great Plains* by Walter Prescott Webb. According to Webb there were no trees out there. It was something I might have known from seeing Western movies with their mesas and cattle drives, but for some reason I found this fact immensely evocative. Into my mind came the image of a vast, barren plain, a rock-strewn universe in which, in the distance, a few stick figures were trying to provide themselves a civilization. My desire to destroy the genre forever turned into a serious engagement with its possibilities: if I would write in counterpoint to its conventions, there would be parody if not in tone then in structure.

All of this came to me in the instant of that image's realization. From the very first sentence I had the voice of the narrator and the situation in which he found himself. None of this was thought out in advance of the writing. I was able to write the book because I had not planned to, and because I was not qualified to, never having been west of Ohio. As a New Yorker I might even have thought Ohio was the West. It was a book that arose solely from the circumstance in which I happened to find myself. *Welcome to Hard Times* is the title under which it was published—a novel set in the Dakota Territory in the 1870s.

I will admit, baldly, that the reviews I received were good enough to certify me as a writer. I thought myself that I'd done a sound piece of work, that I'd pulled it off just as Kafka had in his first novel, *Amerika,* which he wrote without ever having left Prague. And then I received a letter from an elderly lady in Texas. She wrote in a fine, spidery hand, and she said the following: "Young man, I was with you all the way until your Mr. Jenks at his campsite out on the flats made himself a dinner of the roasted haunch of a prairie dog. At that moment I knew you'd probably never been west of

Ohio, because the haunch of a prairie dog wouldn't fill a teaspoon."

Called upon to defend the prerogatives of my art, I replied: "What you say, Madam, may be true of today's prairie dogs. But in the 1870s . . ."

In fact Jenks's hunger might have magnified his measly portion into a dinner. But, right or wrong, I've let the line stand in all subsequent editions of the book. I am leery of perfection. In Hawthorne's great story "The Birthmark," a natural scientist insists on concocting a potion that will erase a birthmark from his beautiful young wife's cheek. He regards it as the one blemish on her perfection. Because she loves him, his wife drinks the potion. The birthmark slowly fades until her beauty is at last perfect. At that moment, she dies. And that's why I have left Jenks still out there on the flats having for dinner a roasted haunch of prairie dog.

My parents were first-generation Americans born in New York City. It was their parents who as young people as yet unmarried arrived separately not at Ellis Island but at Castle Garden in the 1880s, having emigrated from White Russia, now called Belarus. My father's father, Isaac Doctorow, was twenty when he arrived in 1885. He had come over in despair of the life that faced him in Russia, the ever-present murderous whimsy of the pogromists of the time and, more closely and stultifyingly, the rabbinically run village life that demanded fealty to what seemed to him arbitrary ancient proscriptions to induce catatonia, and which offered absolutely no practical means of answering to the poverty and slavery and degradation delivered by the Russian world outside the *shtetl.* Normative Judaism was neither life nor hope for my grandfather, it was praying your way to death.

At any rate, when he was settled in New York, ensconced on the Lower East Side and apprenticed to a printer, he immediately enrolled in a class on socialism taught by a well-known legal scholar of the time, Morris Hillquit, and at the conclusion of the course was rewarded as class valedictorian with the gift of an unabridged dictionary.

By the time I was old enough to know him and think about him, he was elderly and living in the Bronx, a gentle, slim, and handsome man with fine white hair. I. Doctorow was the way he signed his name. He was a retired printer, a chess player—we played chess when I visited—and a voracious reader with a library I was always invited to dip into. Books in English, Russian, and Yiddish. I have mentioned his gift to me of his copy of Tom Paine's *Age of Reason,* that still deliciously eloquent analysis of the Bible's inconsistencies, contradictions, and fantasies; not for Paine the intricate and imaginative work of *midrash.*

(It was something of a mysterious coincidence when, a hundred and fifty-five years after Paine's death, my wife and I bought a house in New Rochelle, New York, that turned out to stand in what had been the apple orchard behind Paine's home there in the 1800s.)

As we sat playing chess my grandfather Isaac was an

island of sweet calm amid the maelstrom of activity going on around him. This maelstrom was my grandmother, Gussie, a tiny sprightly woman who wore her
hair in a crown of braid and who unlike her husband
was devout in her belief. She had come over from the
same village in the Minsk district—they had known
each other casually in the old country and had found
something more going on between them only when
they lived near each other on the Lower East Side. She
was living with her widowed mother when he courted
her. Gussie Doctorow was rigorous in her observances,
kept an impeccably kosher household and went off to
sit upstairs in the synagogue every chance she had. Her
great complaint was that, in her lifelong arguments
about religion with her nonbelieving husband, he
could quote the Bible more accurately than she. And
of course, skeptic or not, I. Doctorow came to my
bar mitzvah and sat there beaming as I read my pas-
sage, which by the way—in the manner of bar mitzvah
preparation in the Bronx in those days—I didn't understand a word of, Hebrew being taught by rote for
memorization with no concern for what the words
meant.

My father Dave was the second of Isaac and Gussie's

three children, and in the life of my own family, of my own father and mother, this same male-female dynamic prevailed. My mother Rose was a musician like her immigrant father before her. As a girl she played the piano for silent movies to earn money for her lessons. She and my father met as teenagers, and after they married in the 1920s they liked to spend their evenings in Greenwich Village—when it was a bohemian quarter alive with poets actors musicians radicals of every stripe. But as they grew older and as life became harder—this was the Depression and my father was by then the struggling proprietor of a music shop—my mother became active in the sisterhood of the local synagogue, and every Friday night she lit the candles and put her hand over her blue eyes and said the blessing and threw in a few silent prayers for good measure. My father never went near the synagogue. He believed like his father that the problems of Earth must be solved on Earth and that religion must not be used as it had been historically as a means of persuading people to live with the misery of social injustice.

It is my belief that the profound incompatibility of opposing ideas expressed in all the complex love flowing to a child of that family was a necessary condition of the child's creativity. He would mature having combined within himself the secular humanism and the impulse to reverence of the male and female lines of his elders. I think of it as a spiritual sort of alternating current, wherein never at rest I swing constantly back and forth from one pole to the other. This is a serendipitous arc for a writer's mind. It describes the less than comfortable state of freedom. As the son of my fathers I am nonobservant, a celebrant of the humanism that has no patience for a religious imagination that asks me to abandon my intellect. But as the son of my mothers, I am unable to discard reverence, however unattached to an object, in recognition that a spontaneously felt sense of the sacred engages the whole human being as the intellect alone cannot.

I understand from biblical scholarship that the Ten Commandments have a generic form—they are modeled on the lord and vassal treaties of ancient Mesopotamia. They are man-made. But I honor the biblical minds who crafted them to structure civilization on an ethically conceived family life—a life that leads us to live in states of moral consequence that, if not yet, may someday bring us closer to a union with, or a truer perception of, what Einstein, with his scrupulously precise scientific humanistic outlook, could only bring himself to call the Old One.

So how has this all played out? Coming of this conflicted articulate household—moneyless, but filled with books and music—I had the privileged childhood of the undogmatized spirit. From the time I began to read, it never occurred to me to wonder about an author's religious background. When I read Jack London and Mark Twain and Charles Dickens, whatever their religious preference might have been never crossed my mind. Were they Christians? Perhaps in some unconscious way I knew that their background was not Jewish. But in fact they were not Christians either, they were Jack London, Mark Twain, and Charles Dickens. And if you think this was a selective blackout on my part, I'll admit that, however strongly circumstantial the evidence may have been, as a high school student I didn't think of Kafka, I. B. Singer, and Saul Bellow as Jews. I thought of them as Kafka, I. B. Singer, and Saul Bellow. I read them and was inspired by them when I was just starting out. But it was never the case of any sort of ethnic bonding with them—they were too spectacularly themselves. Of course the writer's background, religious tradition, nationality, lived life is crucially directive as to what she writes about whom and where . . . but as a reader I find it quite beside the point that García Márquez is a Catholic from Colombia or Jane Austen is an Anglican from Britain, as instrumental as their cultures may have been in forming them. Dostoyevsky is a fanatically orthodox Christian from Russia. What else could he be? But there is another religion the great ones practice in their art, and it has no name.

Or, to change the metaphor, I wonder if great fiction and great poetry are not, down to their deepest roots, secular. W. H. Auden once said that a writer's politics are more of a danger to him than his cupidity. I would add that the writer's religion is as much a danger to him as his politics. Certainly in this country we worry that if a work is formed by ideas exterior to it, if there is some sort of programmed intention, a set of truths to be illustrated, the work will be compromised and will not be art but polemic. We will have corrupted the occasion and betrayed the calling.

Having cut my teeth on the existentialist fictions of Camus and Sartre, I tend to think of them, contrarian as they are, as somehow emblematic of the digging in of the heels that is characteristic of all authorship. As an artifact created of its author's self-differentiation, the successful novel must necessarily lack the humility of reverence, the surrendering quality of the religious spirit. True surrender for an author would find all that needs to be written in the sacred text of his religion. This is clearly not something to occur to Proust, for example. Or even the biblically melancholic Bernard Malamud. I would of course say the same of poets. The Israeli poet Yehuda Amichai went down fighting all the way. Dante, right from the heart of Roman Catholicism, builds his own tripartite version of the afterlife, populates Hell with his Florentine enemies, wanders through it with a pagan mentor, and, most shockingly of all, as the critic Harold Bloom has shown us, exalts Beatrice to the point of blasphemy. And the great devoutly religious poet Gerard Manley Hopkins springs from his palpably elastic lines and image-bouncing bursts of inspiration right up out of Christianity into poetry.

All writers worth the name are unaffiliated. The novelist, the poet, will understand the institutions they live within, including their religious traditions, as aggregate historically amended fictions. Appointing themselves as witnesses, they are necessarily independent of all institutions including the institution of the family—which may be why nothing makes family members more nervous than the discovery that one of them is a writer. They will not quite understand that the writer of the most personalist story, a roman à clef of her own family life or marriage, can be read as protesting the large social structures of the society or the terrible injustice of our brutal ordinary human inadequacy.

However well intentioned, constructive, and generous in spirit it may be to label the work of any group of writers as if their value is first and foremost local, a boon to the neighborhood—as if they are uniformly bound in the cultural context in which they find themselves—to do so runs the risk of portraying them as a chorus, rather than as the soloists, temperamental divas, and unconscionable upstagers that they in fact are. And it seems not to recognize the truth that every author responds to all of the given literature, and that the authorial conversation transcends borders and spans generations.

Of course I understand the hunkering down of all of us into our group loyalties in the past thirty or forty years—there is enough wretchedly catastrophic history behind us to explain why that has happened. I point out that the phrase *political correctness* was originally devised on the political right to mock or defame the effort, even to undermine the desire, of members of ethnic, racial, and gender minorities to articulate their own identities instead of accepting the stereotypical and demeaning identities that history had imposed upon them. In many ways political correctness has been socially constructive. People *should* take pride and satisfaction in who and what they are. The Reconstructionist rabbi Mordecai Kaplan makes the distinction between *separateness* and *otherness*. Ideally it is not separateness but otherness that is practiced when people affirm their roots while warranting themselves as citizens of the larger community. Nevertheless, with all of this said, I think something peculiar—and politically inert—is going on when I walk into a bookstore and see it sectioned off with shelves devoted to gay and lesbian writers, or African-American writers, as if the expected readers for these books can only be gays and lesbians or African Americans, as if the writers of these books have something to say only to gays and lesbians or African Americans, as if Edmund White and Toni Morrison are consumer products, or as if the genres are primary, the writers secondary—as in Inspirational, or Cooking, or Self-Help.

I question any subcultural division of the literary project which I see, in the Emersonian manner, as arising from an unmediated exercise of the lonely mind.

The term *assimilation* as used in the sociological sense refers to a gratifying integration into the great American diaspora, but it may mean as well the disappearance of one's ethnic identity and tradition, a devolution of a rich and complex culture, as Jews marry gentiles, for example, and cease to observe the rituals and practices.

But as I apply the term to literature the meaning is reversed. If I speak of literature as assimilation what is assimilated is the larger culture into the specificity of the book's representations. It is America that is being

ing lately, empowering. I have argued elsewhere that "a sentence spun from the imagination, that is, a sentence composed as a lie, confers on the writer a degree of perception or acuity or heightened awareness that a sentence composed with the strictest attention to fact does not." Why and how this is I don't know, but everyone from the writers of the ancient sacred texts to James himself has relied on that empowering paradox. It involves the working of our linguistic minds on the world of things-in-themselves, when, our perception shot through with memory, our consciousness haunted by dreams, we ascribe meaning to the unmeant and the sentence forms with such synaptic speed that the act of writing, when it is going well, seems no more than the dutiful secretarial response to a silent dictation.

But let's return to the idea that from one fragment of conversation overheard by the writer a whole life and culture can be projected. And of course it can be something else than a conversational fragment, it can be an image, a phrase of music, a felt injustice—any private excitement of the writer's mind so mysteriously evocative that it flowers into a novel. This, in microcosm, reminds me of the Big Bang theory of the origin of the universe, which proposes that from the infinitesimal happenstance of a singular moment/thing the entire universe blew out into its dimensions, exploded in one silent flash into the volume and chronology of space-time.

Is this an outlandish comparison? Perhaps it would be less so if we brought God into the discussion; because if we are made in his image, then it is a truism that every work of art mimics God's cosmic creativity. (In the beginning was The Word.) The Big Bang is our newer more sophisticated though perhaps too flippant metaphor, and the intuitive use of the smallest amount of information to create a fictional world suggests more accurately, more precisely the little bang of the writer's inspiration. And if we recall Emerson's faculty of reporting (that's us) and the possibility of being reported (that's the universe), clearly the origin of the universe and the origin of every reported universe in the mind of the writer are isodynamic.

I'm satisfied that the ancient storytellers of the oral tradition, whose systematic fictions were to be eventually recorded in the sacred texts, would have attributed those fictions, or their inspiration, to God, would have attributed to God the consequential revelatory under-standings that come of the practice of storytelling when it is done righteously, that is, in the belief that it is a system of knowledge.

Therefore, when I speak of the narratives of the Judeo-Christian heritage as fictions, and their histori-cal communities of believers as fiction readers given, in Coleridge's phrase, to a "willing suspension of disbe-lief," I am not speaking pejoratively, I am speaking as a writer about writing and reading, one who knows and can attest to the power of the not entirely rationally de-rived truths of good storytelling to affect mass con-sciousness and create moral constituencies.

With no feeling of irreverence, I can think of the biblical authors as colleagues because it is apparent that their devotion to God did not preclude the use of narrative strategies. Very often, and certainly in mys-tery stories, the writer works backward. The ending is known and the story is designed to arrive at the end-ing. If you know the people of the world speak many languages, that is the ending. The story of the Tower of Babel gets you there. The known ending of life is death. The story of Adam and Eve in the Garden of Eden arrives at that ending—the human condition is turned into a sequential narrative of how it came to be. The narrative tropes, conflicting forces, fatal choices, denouement, create a moral framework for *being*. And in suggesting that things might have worked out another way for humanity if the fruit of the Tree of Knowledge had not been eaten, this wonderful story, not incidentally, left itself open to revision by a subsequent fantasist who would read into it the idea of original sin.

Another venerable storytelling practice is the appropriation of an already existing story. Otherwise known as adaptation, it is the principle of literary communalism that allows us to use other peoples' myths, legends, and histories in a way to serve ourselves. The writers of Genesis have retold the story of the Flood from earlier Mesopotamian and Sumerian tales, including the vivid rendition in the Epic of Gilgamesh. The plot may be the same, of course, but the meanings are different as befits adaptation. Noah is unprecedented as the last God-fearing man on earth . . . who may nevertheless drink a bit more than is good for him. And the God of Genesis is a Presence beyond the conception of the Sumerian epic.

The cosmology of Genesis is supremely beautiful

storytelling, and for all we know may even turn out to be as metaphorically prescient as some believers think it is. One imagines the ancient storytellers convening to consider what they had to work with: day and night, earth and sky, land and sea, trees that bore fruit, plants that bore seed, wild animals, domesticated animals, birds, fish, and everything that crept. In their brilliant imaginations, inflamed by the fear and love of God, it seemed more than possible that these elements and forms of life, this organization of the animate and in-animate, would have been produced from a chaos of indeterminate dark matter by spiritual intent—here was the story to get to the ending—and that it would have been a process of discretion, the separation of day from night, air from water, earth from sky, one thing from another in an elegant six-day sequence culminat-ing in the supreme achievement of the writers them-selves.

As to literary strategies, it is the invention of charac-ter that is most telling, and in Genesis it is God who is the most complex and riveting character, at times as troubled and conflicted and as moved by the range of human feelings as the human beings he has created.

The personality of God cannot be an entirely unwitting set of traits in a theological text that declares we are made in his image.

In the Bible, character is fate. And life under God is always an allegory.

WHY WE ARE INFIDELS

We have lately been called infidels. Yet we are perhaps the most prayerful nation in the world. Both Tocqueville and Dickens when they came over here to have a look at us were astonished at how much God there was in American society. True, the infidel is not necessarily a nonbeliever; he may also be a believer of the wrong stripe. But I think, given the variety of religious practice in our country, including that of Islam, that the term *infidel* as it has lately been applied to us probably does not refer to any particular religion we may as a nation subscribe to, but to the fact that we subscribe, within our population of three hundred million, to all of them.

Of course most of our religions, including Christianity, Judaism, Islam, Buddhism, landed here at different times from other parts of the world. They have been vulnerable as religions usually are to such denominational fracture as to offer a potential parishioner a virtual supermarket of spiritual choice. Some of our religions, Mormonism, Christian Science, Native American Anthropomorphism, were invented, or revealed, right here. And if we think even casually of the parade of creative and influential religionists on our shores—from the colonists Anne Hutchinson and Roger Williams, George Fox, Jonathan Edwards, and Cotton Mather to our citizen evangelicals Aimee Semple Mc-Pherson, Billy Sunday, Father Divine, and Billy Graham, we notice immediately that we have left out the Adventists, the Millerites, the Shakers, Swedenborgians, and Perfectionists of the nineteenth century, to say nothing of the stadium-filling brides and grooms of the Reverend Moon's Unification Church, or the suicidal cultists of Jim Jones, or the unfortunate Branch Davidians of Waco, Texas, or the Heaven's Gate believers who castrated themselves and took their own lives in order to board the Hale-Bopp comet when it flew past in 1997.

One of the less scintillating debates among theologians is on the distinction between a religion and a cult. But all together, our religions or religious cults testify to the deeply serious American thirst for celestial connection. We want a spiritual release from the society we have made out of secular humanism.

That our God-soaked country is, as political science, secular, may be indicated by the fact that the word for the state of being of an infidel, *infidelity,* brings to our minds not a violation of faith in the true God but a violation of the marriage contract between ordinary mortals. Philandering husbands and adulterous wives may be viewed as immoral and looked upon with contempt or pity, but they are not usually regarded as infidels. The term however may be justly applied to all of us, including the most pious and monogamous among us, because of a major national sin committed over two hundred years ago when religion and the American state were rent asunder and all worship was consigned to private life. It was Jefferson who said, "Our civil rights have no dependence on our religious opinions, any more than our opinions in physics or geometry." And while it is precisely because of this principle of religious freedom that we enjoy such a continuous national uproar of praying and singing and studying and fasting and confessing and atoning and praising and preaching and dancing and dunking and vowing and quaking and shaking and abstaining and ordaining, a paradox arises from this expression of our religious democracy: if you have extracted the basic ethics of religious invention and found the mechanism for installing them in the statutes of the secular civil order, as we have with our Constitution and our Bill of Rights, but have consigned all the doctrine and rite and ritual, all the symbols and traditional practices to the precincts of private life, you are saying there is no one proven path to salvation, there are only traditions. If you relegate the old stories to the personal choices of private worship, you admit the ineffable is ineffable, and in terms of a possible theological triumphalism everything is up for grabs.

Our pluralism has to be a profound offense to the fundamentalist who by definition is an absolutist intolerant of all forms of belief but his own, all stories but his own. In our raucous democracy fundamentalist religious belief has organized itself with political acumen to promulgate law that would undermine just those secular humanist principles that encourage it to flourish in freedom. Of course there has rarely been a period in our history when God has not been called upon to march. The abolitionists decried slavery as a sin against God. The South claimed biblical authority for its slave-holding. The civil disobedience of Dr. Martin Luther King Jr.'s civil rights movement drew its strength from prayer and the examples of Christian fortitude, while the Ku Klux Klan and other white supremacy groups invoked Jesus as a sponsor of their racism. But there is a crucial difference of emphasis between these traditional invocations and the politically astute and well-funded actions in recent years of the leaders of the movement known as the Christian Right, who do not call upon their faith to certify their politics as much as they call for a country that certifies their faith.

Fundamentalism really cannot help itself—it is absolutist and can compromise with nothing, not even democracy. It is not surprising that immediately after the Islamic fundamentalist attack on the World Trade Center and the Pentagon two prominent Christian fundamentalists were reported to have accounted it as justifiable punishment by God for our secularism, our civil libertarianism, our feminists, our gay and lesbian citizens, our abortion providers, and everything and everyone else which their fundamentalist belief con-

THE POLITICS OF GOD

We do not necessarily have to embrace the secular glories of modernism—which include nuclear weapons, environmental ruin, and relentlessly impersonal economic structures that have produced mass poverty and severe forms of alienation in many parts of the world—to see that, for the religious extremist, the idea of the sacred is implanted in the same antediluvian circuits of the brain where reside our tribal fears and hatreds. How, given the increasingly warlike pietism around the world since the end of the Cold War, can we avoid concluding that fundamentalism is the truest expression of the religious sensibility? Compared to the self-sacrifice of religiously inspired suicide bombers, what shall we say of the drift away from literalism in contemporary Christianity and Judaism and Islam, the acceptance of the concept of scriptural events as having metaphorical rather than literal truth, for example, or the opening up of the liturgical privilege to women and gays, or the renunciation of female drapery, or the sociological emphasis on community welfare, or the reengineering of the religious words by theologians to accommodate everything the secular intellect has taught us? What can we say of such enlightened developments in the past hundred years or so except that they are condemned by literalists, with some justice, as dilutions, as enervations, as *not religious enough?* The religious modality may now be declaring itself tenable only in its simple, atavistic readings of the ancient texts. So that, finally, true fulfillment of the prophecies is not possible except in the pure form of the theocratic state.

We must honor the achievements of religious inspiration in human history. Withal, there has always been something about the organized attention to God that is wrongly proprietary, with a sharp murderous edge to it. It is as if piety itself has a flawed circuit that tends to blow, and the devotion to God becomes the will to power. Nietzsche so characterized Christianity, recognizing the reactive humility of turning the other cheek, for example, as one of the most powerful political acts imaginable. If we look at the beginnings of Christianity, the dispute between those gospelers who, somewhat mystical or gnostic in nature, rejected the idea of an authoritarian priesthood (and were ultimately heretical), and the synoptic gospelers (ultimately canonical), whose principle of apostolic succession was their chosen means of assuring the survival of the faith in the Roman world . . . it was a politicized Jesus created from that conflict, and it has been a politicized Jesus ever since, from the time of the Roman emperor Constantine's conversion in the fourth century through the long history of European Christianity, with its crusades, its inquisitions, its demonization of Jews, its contests and/or alliances with kings and emperors, and, with the rise of the Reformation, its active participation in all its forms in the wars among states and the rule of populations.

We don't have to resort to the long historical view—the biblical disputes between Pharisees and Essenes of ancient Israel—in order to note that in Israel today small parties of the super orthodox have cited their biblical right to establish settlements in the West Bank, and in fact, continue to deem it God's will to install their own religious practices as laws for all Israelis. Perhaps in this context too we're justified in recalling the

pious Jewish fundamentalism of the assassin of the Israeli prime minister Yitzhak Rabin.

The late Taliban rulers of Afghanistan controlled all
private life in that country—banning education for female children, issuing edicts concerning dress, reading
material, dancing, laying down a whole blanket of pro-
hibitions on the private lives of the population according to their religious ideals which, not incidentally,
they had affirmed with their assault rifles and rocket
launchers.

I'm aware this is a secular humanist canticle I'm
singing, and perhaps of no real relevance to the person
of faith whose life shines with decent and well-meant
conduct and whose being is healthy with joyous conviction. I admit that I can't listen to good gospel singing in an African-American church without wanting to
join in, without acknowledging the strength and dig-
nity and self-realization it confers. And when I see a
young family, mother and father and small children
holding their hands, all of them dressed in their Saturday best as they walk to their synagogue, I feel a sweet
envy for the peace and order and resolution of their tradition keeping. But when I am moved by religious

worship, it is by its innocence and trust. That innocence and trust always seems to carry with it the idea of promise, it seems to me a necessarily provisional state, a prayerful waiting, as if, given our knowledge of the unthinkable horrors brought down upon our forebears, and the ordinary suffering to which we are all subject, we seek the finally effective prayer, the hymn that will be heard, and hold ourselves to the resolute belief in God that may someday actually bring him into being.

Is it possible that the terrorism of the most devout and self-martyring Muslim has, at its heart, that same provisional and so even more despairing hope? Apart from the rare experience of ecstatic revelation, the religious commitment is a matter of education—some would say indoctrination—or family loyalty, or conversion inspired by political bitterness. Does the leap of faith ever land? It does for the prophet, the revelator, but for whom else? Freud in *The Future of an Illusion* speaks to this point:

If the truth of religious doctrines is dependent on an inner experience which bears witness to that truth, what is one to do about the many people who do not have this rare experience? One may require every man to use the gifts of reason which he possesses, but one cannot erect, on the basis of a motive that exists only for a very few, an obligation that shall apply to everyone. If one man has gained an unshakeable conviction of the true reality of the religious doctrines from a state of ecstasy which has deeply moved him, of what significance is that to others?

The secular intellect is self-liberating and has been flourishing exponentially in the Western world for the last five hundred years. It needs no preachers, it is generative and self-revelatory, unlike the God of our scriptures. It won't stop now, it can't. The modernist project has endowed mankind with the scientific method, the concept of objective evidence, the culture of factuality responsible for the good and extended life we enjoy in the high-tech world of our freedom, but more important for the history of our species, the means to whatever verified knowledge we have regarding the nature of life and the origins and laws of the physical world. But it does not, historically, turn out to have been of universal benefit. It too has a politics, no less brutal if far less ecstatic—currently a trans-national politics of corporate imperialism. It may be more abstract, and with its devastations as likely to be slow and eroding as swift and bloody, but it leaves as many millions impoverished, enslaved, and wasted, and with greater efficiency, as did the holy wars of old.

We could here acknowledge the continuum of evil in human affairs and find distinctions only in the justifying terminology. But this would be to succumb to Augustine's self-serving and regressive idea of original sin. The fact is that since the providing genius of the ancient texts of thousands of years ago, the rare moral advances of the human race have come not of religious but of secular institutions. The concept of democracy and its attendant freedoms was one such advance. The perception of the earth as a destructible environment is another. Declared universal human rights and the international war crimes tribunal are other such budding advances.

Suffering is not necessarily a moral endowment. Those to whom evil is done do evil. If radical fundamentalism arises from despair of the modernist project, its failures, its social sicknesses, its blatant exclusions, clearly the solution, too, must come from modernism. There are no religious remedies for the secular diseases of want and disenfranchisement, there are only secular remedies. Were the United States and other Western democracies to embark on an economic program to ease the poverty of populations in the Near and Far East—it would have to be one with a far different ethos from that of the World Trade Organization and the World Bank, which are seen, correctly, by poor working people around the world as instruments of their oppression—and were we to disentangle ourselves from those authoritarian regimes we prop up for our own economic ends, then presumably the recruiting pool for suicidal bombers and nihilist jihadists would dry up. Or would it? That result is far from certain because among the more radical movements Western individualism is a profound blasphemy for which there is no atonement. Also, despots who, in league with their clerical establishments, encourage religious extremism do not particularly want to alleviate poverty and ignorance—the good life as promoted by Western democracies threatens their rule. But what is certain is that the principle of mutual assured destruction that served as a deterrent in the Cold War will not deter aspiring religious martyrs with visions of their own celestial glory. So apart from any moral imperative we might have to ease suffering and alleviate injustice, doing that may also be the only practicable course for the modernist societies. And it is at least conceivable that this strange period of atavistic energies, when what is very old is very new, as if time is a loop, would lose its momentum, and eventually even the most fanatic keepers of the faith might have to consider why all human knowledge since scripture is not also God's revelation.

The question then becomes whether what is possible is probable.

pia. The ratification parades were sacramental—symbolic venerations, acts of faith. From the beginning people saw the Constitution as a kind of sacred text for a civil society.

Every written composition has a voice, a persona, a character of self-presentation. The voice of our Constitution is a quiet voice. (I have taken the trouble to read it and have elsewhere written in some detail about this.) It is not a call to arms like the Declaration of Independence. It is a voice that does not argue, explain, condemn, excuse, or rationalize. Not claiming righteousness, it is however suffused with rectitude; its operative verb is *shall.* As in "all legislative powers herein granted shall be vested in a Congress of the United States which shall consist of a Senate and a House of Representatives." The Constitution gives law and assumes for itself the power endlessly to give law. It ordains. It is cold, distant, remote, as a voice from on high, self-authenticating. The voice of the Constitution is the inescapably solemn self-consciousness of the people giving the law unto themselves. But since, in the Judeo-Christian world of Western civilization, all given law imitates God, the ultimate lawgiver, the voice of the Constitution is the voice of scripture. The ordaining voice of the Constitution is scriptural, but in resolutely keeping the authority for its dominion in the public consent, it presents itself as the sacred text of secular humanism.

It is true of the sacred texts of the world's great religions that a body of additional law and commentary has built up around the source material that also achieves the force of prophecy. The Torah has its Talmud, the Koran its Hadith, the New Testament its apostolic teachings. We have our sacred secular humanist amendments, as well as the commentaries or interpretive decisions of the federal courts which themselves have the authority of law because the Constitution must be applied to a multitude of situations. And where the prophecy has been false the country has seen turmoil. The hideous Article Four that made a slave in one state a slave in all brought on the national calamity of a civil war.

Today, the Constitution with its Bill of Rights and further amendments rules us with a set of behavioral proscriptions that, if we lived up to all of them, would make us a truly free and righteous people. When the ancient Hebrews broke their covenant they suffered a loss of identity and brought disaster on themselves.

Our burden too is unmistakably covenantal. We may point to our two hundred some years of national survival as an open society, constitutionally sworn to a degree of free imaginative expression that few cultures in the world can tolerate, we may regard ourselves as an exceptionalist historically self-correcting nation whose democratic values locate us just as surely as our geography . . . and yet we know at the same time that all through our history we have brutally excluded vast numbers of us from the shelter of the New Roof, we have broken our covenant again and again with a virtuosity verging on damnation and have been saved only by the sacrificial efforts of Constitution-reverencing patriots in government and out of government—presidents, senators, justices, self-impoverishing lawyers, abolitionists, muckrakers, third party candidates, suffragists, union organizers, striking workers, civil rights martyrs.

I would not want it inferred, from my invidious comparison of fundamentalist belief with the civil religious culture of the country, that the establishment of a constitutional republic has delivered us from evil.

As Washington is run today, major issues of public policy are bent to the desires of those who control the Congress with their money. Time and time again socially desirable legislation in the public interest—whether having to do with health care, public safety, environmental protection, preservation of our natural resources, or any other issue of clear relevance to the entire society—is defeated, or sabotaged with statutory language into its perverse opposite. This is the recurrent truth of Washington, so rhythmically repetitive as to be its heartbeat. Business entities that pit themselves against the manifest needs of the American people, according to the issues that arise, take turns as enemies of the people. Nothing else on Capitol Hill occurs so reliably and regularly. This political fact of life is hardly news. It has been a long long time since it was news. It is now only and obviously the way things are.

Corporate interests that function in Washington to achieve benefits for themselves—tax loopholes, entitlements, privileged access to natural resources, deregulation of regulatory acts—regardless of the overall social effect, preempt the idea of the larger community, the national ideal, the United States as the ultimate communal reality. A just nation is not envisioned, but a confederacy whose denizens are meant to live at the expense of one another. Such social Darwinism finds the ideals of democracy naive.

A prominent senator said a few years ago, as he sponsored legislation written by corporate lobbyists, that after all they were the specialists in their field who knew the issues better than anyone else. This can only be the statement of a politician not in public service but in service to those who run the country for themselves, a politician confident of a general population so numbed and alienated that a majority does not bother to vote in national elections. These are the flaunted values of a politician who knows of the conglomerate-owned media that there will be no editorial muckraking from the "in depth" journalists of the television screen, that the plutocratic character of the present state of government will not be defined for what it is, and that anyone who speaks of the bewildering broad front of failure and mendacity and carelessness of human life in so much of our public policy in tones any louder than muted regret will be marginalized for this indecorous transgression as a leftist, or perhaps a raging populist, but in any event someone so out of the "mainstream" as not to be taken seriously.

Given the prevailing rules of the game, it is not surprising that we are compromising the ideal of public education, privatizing our prisons for profit, despoiling the environment, and conglomerating all forms of communication, books and magazines and newspapers and radio stations and cable TV channels, movies, and music, into one smooth reality-laundering revenue stream that is in fact a ready-made highly suggestive simulacrum of state-controlled media.

To consider the elected politician in all of this is to mourn the days when amateurism was part of the political culture. One can acknowledge the integrity and honesty of many elected officials while knowing that for some of them, enough of them, their political vision extends only as far as the outer tables of their fund-raising dinners. To hear the points of view of some of these people—how thoroughly they have become the forces that have bought them—is to realize they are no longer guilty of hypocrisy, having been transmogrified. The instructive image is from Dante's *Inferno,* Canto XXV. We are in a pouch of the Eighth Circle, where the thieves reside. A typical transaction occurs between a thief and one of Hell's manifestations, in this case a monstrous six-legged lizard-like creature who leaps onto a thief, wraps its middle feet around his belly, pins his two arms with its forelegs, and, wrapping its rear feet around his knees, swings its tail up between his legs and sinks its teeth into his face. And so intertwined, monster and thief, they begin to melt into one another like hot wax, their two heads joining, their substances merging, until a new third creature is created though somehow redolent of both of them. And it slowly slithers away into the darkness.

As we find ourselves today with a president elected under questionable circumstances, and implications of shadowy secret dealings between his administration's officials and sleazy business interests, and with a federal judiciary thick with right-wing justices engaged in rescinding legislative responses to the inequities of past generations, I wonder, with all of this, if I am the only one to find my country increasingly difficult to recognize. Given the threat of international terrorism, measures endorsed by the Congress, under presidential goading, call for secret military tribunals, abrogate the confidential relations between legal defendants and their counsel, allow indeterminate periods of incommunicado detention for people suspected of crimes, and install legal means for the secret surveillance and secret searches of the homes and offices of persons who come for one reason or another under official suspicion.

I have to ask if this rage to deconstruct the Constitution and the Bill of Rights has any connection with the prevalence of God in our political discourse. It is never less than a companionable relationship so many of our politicians claim to have with God. For some this relationship is more a political expedient than anything else. For others it is presumably sincere. In either case, I wonder to what extent, and at however unconscious a level, a conflict arises in the political mind when it is sworn to uphold the civil religion of the Constitution.

Undeniably, enormous metaphysical risks come with the heritage of the Enlightenment. The comfort of a church God does relieve us of such risks.

To take the long view, American politics may be seen as the struggle between the idealistic secular democracy of a fearlessly self-renewing America, the metaphysical risks that are the heritage of the Enlightenment, and our great resident capacity to be in denial of what it is intellectually and morally incumbent upon us to pursue.

Melville in *Moby-Dick* speaks of "reality outracing apprehension." Apprehension in the sense not of fear or disquiet but of understanding . . . reality as too much for us to take in, as, for example, the white whale is too much for the *Pequod* and its captain. It may be that our new century is an awesome complex white whale swiftly outracing our understanding—scientifically in our quantumized wave/particles and the manipulable stem cells of our biology, ecologically in our planetary crises of nature, technologically in our humanoid molecular computers, sexually in the rising number of our genders, intellectually in the paradoxes of our texts, and so on.

What we can rely on are the saving powers of simplism. Perhaps with our dismal public conduct, so shot through with piety, we are actually engaged in a genetic-engineering venture that will make a slower, dumber, more sluggish whale, one that can be harpooned and flensed, tried and boiled to light our candles. A kind of water-wonderworld whale made of racism, nativism, cultural illiteracy, fundamentalist fantasy, and the righteous priorities of wealth.

I remind myself of the strength of this federal republic that has managed to survive more than two centuries of abuse at the hands of its citizens. To do this I have to avoid thinking of the immense human losses we have taken, the profligacy of death in a nation that, like Nature, can seem to take all sorts of losses and still go on. Yet a love of country and a faith in its immense promise can allow us to recognize of our civil religion that, unlike the God religions, it draws no fixed line between inclusion and exclusion, between salvation and damnation. Our American civil religion oscillates, expands and contracts periodically, to include or exclude, as its own controlling forces find necessary, to bless or to damn according to its economic contingencies, its crises of war, its dolors of peace, and, above all, the character of those who, constitutionally or not, have assumed ruling powers.

This is small consolation to the sufferer of one or another kind of deep, socially inflicted misfortune who discovers that suffering is distinctive and does not migrate from soul to soul. But it is something to hold on to. Behind our political disfigurement the presumptions of democracy endure. We are indebted as Americans to an underlying civil religion that accounts for the exceptionalism we claim as a nation. A civil society can evolve. A theocracy cannot.

Terrorism may be the word that will, in time, come to describe not merely the stateless (if state-sponsored) random acts of murder and destruction directed against political democracies, as it does now, but an alliance of theocratic despotisms confronting us as critically as Lenin's communism and Hitler's fascism confronted us in the last century. The politics of God are an ancient and time-tested means of mobilizing masses of people. Theocratic rulers may use religion cynically to maintain their power, but their societies are capable of an ideological intensity that leaves a secular nation at a disadvantage. The fundamentalists display a fierce self-knowledge, whereas we, in the complexities of our social compact, in our freedom and our variousness, seem never quite willing to affirm the metaphysical basis of our society. (Paradoxically, they seem to understand our meaning more clearly than we do—it is what they detest.) After September 11, 2001, our politicians resolved to destroy the criminal conspiracy of Al Qaeda, but other than "God Bless America" and the familiar evocations of our democratic heritage, they did not articulate the reality that, apart from our self-romancing, makes us what we are, and proposes what we mean to the history of civilization.

The idea of the United States may have had its sources in the European Enlightenment, but it was the actions taken by self-declared Americans that brought it into focus and established it as an entity. America is a society evolved from words written down on paper by ordinary mortals, however extraordinary they happened to be as human beings. Constitutional scholars are accustomed to speak metaphorically of our American civil religion, as though two hundred or so years ago something happened only in terms of our national history. But along with its separation of church and state, our Constitution with its Amendments adapted as the basis of civil law what are essentially the ethical proscriptions common to Judaism, Christianity, and Islam. There was not only a separation but an appropriation which goes largely unremarked and is consequential not just in our national history but in human history.

Freed from state endorsement, our mainstream religious traditions have slowly, with much backing and filling, liberalized themselves—a process that has, in turn, provoked the rise of evangelical and fundamentalist movements that are defiantly orthodox. As an old piece of furniture is stripped of its paint and the raw wood is exposed, so has the ecstatic literalism that is the truth of the religious modality been exposed. It is possible to see that the entireness of the ancient system of life under God has been compromised, the ethics absorbed into the civic culture, the *mysterium tremendum* of kneeling and self-prostrating worship left in freedom to those who would have it.

And what is the result? In our time it is no more likely that a religious person will live a moral life than that an irreligious person will. In fact it may be that the advocates of the unchangeable doctrine, the censors, the guardians of the sacred texts, the intolerantly righteous, of whatever tradition, are in spirit as well as action less God fearing than the average secular individual in a modern constitutional democracy who has quietly accepted and installed in himself or herself the best ethical teachings of religious traditions. In this view, the moral authority is not God who is prayed to, pleaded with, portrayed, textualized, or given voice, choir, or sacrament, but God who is imperceptible, if not dubious, *except for our evolved moral sense of ourselves.*

We may ask if it is possible that the ethical commandments of religion can be maintained without reference to God. The traditional answer is no—there can be no *ought,* no categorical imperative in the Kantian sense, no action from an irresistible conscience, without a supreme authority. But this conclusion may be begging the question if, as seems likely, God is hidden in its premise.

Here is what Albert Einstein, in *Out of My Later Years,* has to say of the matter:

Ethical axioms are found and tested not very differently from the axioms of science. Truth is what stands the test of experience . . . For pure logic all axioms are arbitrary, including the axioms of ethics. But they are by no means arbitrary from a psychological and genetic point of view. They are derived from our inborn tendencies to avoid pain and annihilation, and from the accumulated emotional reaction of individuals to the behavior of their neighbors . . . It is the privilege of man's moral genius . . . to advance ethical axioms which are so comprehensive and so well founded that men will accept them as grounded in the vast mass of their individual emotional experiences.

In the course of my own life I have observed that the great civilizer on earth seems to have been doubt. Doubt, the constantly debated and flexible inner condition of theological uncertainty, the wish to believe in balance with rueful or nervous or grieving skepticism, seems to have held people in thrall to ethical behavior, while the true believers of whatever stamp, religious or religious statist, have done the murdering. The impulse to exclude, satanize, eradicate, is a religious impulse. But to hold in abeyance and irresolution any firm convictions of God, or of an afterlife with him, warrants walking in his spirit, somehow.

The philosopher Richard Rorty has suggested in his book *Achieving Our Country* that the metaphysic of America's civil religion is pragmatism and its prophets are Walt Whitman and John Dewey. "The most striking feature of their redescription of our country is its thoroughgoing secularism," says Rorty. "The moral

[they] draw from the European past, and in particular from Christianity, is not instruction about the authority under which we should live, but suggestions about how to make ourselves wonderfully different from anything that has been."

To temporize human affairs, to look not up for some applied celestial accreditation, but forward, at ground level, in the endless journey, to resist any authoritarian restriction on thought—that is the essence of the civil religion.

Yet though I subscribe to the pragmatist metaphysic of democracy I part company with its insistence that there can be no immanent teleology—no indwelling supernal plan, as the oak dwells in the acorn—in the affairs of mankind. I understand this is a contradiction, which a true pragmatist could not logically abide. On the other hand, I can sniff out absolutist thinking even in the best of propositions. I do not ignore Whitman's advice (as quoted in Rorty) to "be not curious about God" if I find that it is at least possible for a teleology to be lateral, moving forward with us in time, or if I suggest that God can in some way be reformulated, progressively, through the expansive human inquiry that, through the generations, will still see humankind putting all the work and responsibility for the value of life on its own shoulders.

Is not Emerson's finally the freest and least dogmatic formulation of pragmatism?

. . . all that can be thought can be written . . . a man is the faculty of reporting, and the universe is the possibility of being reported.

Suppose then that in the context of an enlightened secularism, the idea of God might be recognized as Something Evolving, as civilization evolves—that God can be redefined and recast as the human race trains itself to a greater metaphysical and scientific sophistication. With the understanding, in other words, that human history does show the pattern at least of a progressive sophistication of metaphors. So that we pursue a purposive God that thus far, in the universe as vast as the perceivable cosmos, and as infinitesimal as a subatomic particle, has given us only the one substantive indication of Itself—that we, as humans, do, in fact, live in morally consequential states of being.

Dare we hope that the theologians might liberate

themselves, so as to articulate or perceive another possibility for us in our quest for the sacred? Not just a new chapter, but a new story?

Or are they the embodiment of another light that has failed?

There may not be much time. If the demographers are right, ten billion people will inhabit the Earth by the middle of this century. Sprawling mega-cities and enormous flows of refugees fighting for the resources of the planet. People struggling in sacral hope not to be commodified . . . and perhaps with only the time-tested politics of God and the waging of his holy wars to see them through. Under these circumstances, the prayers of mankind will sound to Heaven as shrieks. And we will have such abuses, such shocks to our hope of what life can be, as to make the blood-soaked, incinerated century just past a paradise lost.

LITERATURE AS RELIGION

I return to a picture of myself as a child, reading. I could not have understood reading as an act of faith. I could not have supposed that every time I removed a book from the library shelf and held it out to the librarian for her stamp, I was enacting a sacrament. Nor later, as a college student, could I have conceived the great American writers of the nineteenth century as *de facto* prophets created by their new country to speak in its voice. The proprieties of literary criticism would not allow such romancing. But the Americanness of Poe, Thoreau, Emerson, Whitman, Dickinson, Mark Twain is not merely a matter of geography. While the vast acreage of the New World might suggest a magnitude for the human imagination inconceivable to a European, there is something perhaps more crucial to the American nationality of these writers. They were not that far removed in time from the impertinent revolution and the still breathtaking social reality of a land severed from kingship and so from the lineage claimed by kings. These writers understood freedom as unencumbered though perhaps unblessed by an ecclesiastical culture. Their personalities differed, and in literary address and in what interested them they couldn't have been more diverse. But each of their minds saw through to the metaphysical disquiet that comes with a Democracy. And whether in pain, or gloom, or elation or morbidity or bitter satire, they accepted it. The reportage of these nineteenth-century authors teases out the ontological premises of the Enlightenment. Whatever their religious hopes or conflicts might have been, as writers they prophesy the American future implicit, if not entirely intentional, in the formative documentations of the Founding Fathers.

They could disdain the democratic mob around them, as did Poe, who, given all that room, all that sky and air, sent his words out from the sealed crypt of his own brain; or they could open their arms as rhapsodists, theologically self-infatuated from the use of words, which was the case with Emerson (the critic Alfred Kazin calls Emerson an "orphic writer," and quotes Emerson's allusion to Jesus as a poet whose tropes were wrongly literalized by history). They could be self-consecrating, as Walt Whitman certainly was, all his life the singer of himself. Twain, unlike Hawthorne, did not find the tragedy in churchly rectitude; he was a merciless skeptic for whom the ordinary pieties were a form of fraud. Emily Dickinson uses her words as stitches, as if life is a garment that needs mending. And in Herman Melville—well, there the reportage most dramatically anticipates much of the twentieth century's. He is an anthropologist of religion and sees the gods of savages as no less legitimate than his god. The universe he reports is as amoral and monstrous as the featureless megalithic head of the white whale. The color white, traditionally linked to purity, is for him the color of evil, colorless itself but, as light, giving the colors of "a harlot" to the natural world.

All of these voices together, were they one, would suggest a bipolar mental disorder. Nevertheless they comprise the demanding literary project of a secular nation.

I come back, in conclusion, to Whitman. Our great poet and pragmatic philosopher advises us not to be curious about God but to affix our curiosity to our own ground-level lives and the earth we live on and then perhaps as far as we can see into the universe with our telescopes. This was the charge he gave himself, and it is the source of all the attentive love in his poetry: If we accept it as our own and decide something is right after all in a democracy that is given to a degree of free imaginative expression that few cultures in the world can tolerate, we can hope for the aroused witness, the manifold reportage, that will restore us to ourselves, awaken the dulled senses of our people to the public interest that is their interest, and vindicate the genius of the humanist sacred text that embraces us all.

Whitman when he walked the streets of New York loved everything he saw—the multitudes that thrilled him, the industries at work, the ships in the harbor, the clatter of horses and carriages, the crowds in the streets, the flags of celebration. Yet he knew, of course, that the newspaper business from which he made his living relied finally for its success on the skinny shoulders of itinerant newsboys, street urchins who lived on the few cents they made hawking the papers in every corner of the city. Thousands of vagrant children lived in the streets of the city that Whitman loved. Yet his exultant optimism and awe of human achievement was not demeaned; he could carry it all, the whole city, and attend like a nurse to its illnesses but like a lover to its fair face.

And so must we.

ACKNOWLEDGMENTS

I am indebted to Mary Bahr and Jason Epstein for their cogent critiques of the manuscript. I thank Margaretta Fulton of Harvard University Press for her editorial counsel and her patience. Camille Smith, Senior Editor, steered the book unerringly through production. Professor Morton Horwitz of Harvard Law School arranged the visit of this Massey Lecturer with collegial grace.